DAILY DEVOTIONAL AND JOURNAL
A 40-DAY PERSONAL JOURNEY

JIM W. GOLL

THE Seer

THE PROPHETIC POWER
OF VISIONS, DREAMS, AND
OPEN HEAVENS

Text compiled by Jan Sherman.

Destiny Image® Publishers, Inc.
P.O. Box 310
Shippensburg, PA 17257-0310

*"Speaking to the Purposes of God for This Generation
and for the Generations to Come"*

ISBN 0-7684-2295-7

For Worldwide Distribution
Printed in the U.S.A.

This book and all other Destiny Image, Revival Press, MercyPlace, Fresh Bread, Destiny Image Fiction, and Treasure House books are available at Christian bookstores and distributors worldwide.

1 2 3 4 5 6 7 8 9 10 / 09 08 07 06 05

Call toll-free:
1-800-722-6774.

For more information on foreign distributors, call
717-532-3040.

Or reach us on the Internet:
www.destinyimage.com

Table of Contents

Seer and Prophet: Two Prophetic Streams

BEFORE I FORMED YOU IN THE WOMB I KNEW YOU, AND BEFORE YOU WERE BORN I CONSECRATED YOU; I HAVE APPOINTED YOU A PROPHET TO THE NATIONS.

(JEREMIAH 1:5)

In the spiritual realm, the flow of the prophetic from Heaven to earth resembles the Nile River. Just as the White Nile and the Blue Nile join to create the greater river called the Egyptian Nile, two streams of prophetic anointing come together to feed the greater concourse of the mighty prophetic river of God on earth. We can call these two streams the stream of the *prophet* and the *stream* of the seer.

Another way to look at this is to turn it around and think of a great prophetic river flowing from the throne of God that breaks into two streams—the *prophet* and the *seer*—which then give different degrees or dimensions or facets of prophetic impartation. Either way, it should be clear that both streams are important for the full expression of the Lord's prophetic word to His people in our day.

What is the difference between a *prophet* and a *seer?…all true seers are prophets but not all prophets are seers….*

A prophet or prophetess, then, is a spokesperson for God; one who hears the voice of the Holy Spirit and speaks or pens God's mind or counsel through a "divinely anointed manner."

(Quote From *The Seer*, Pages 17-19)

QUESTIONS

1. From your understanding, how did God choose Old Testament prophets? Did they have to meet certain qualifications?

2. List five examples of Old Testament prophets. Look them up in the Bible and tell how God called each of them into service as a prophet or seer.

3. Why do you think God determined to have two streams of His great prophetic river? Have you seen these two streams in operation today?

4. The author tells us that "all true seers are prophets but not all prophets are seers." What do you think this means?

5. How does a prophet or prophetess hear the voice of the Holy Spirit? Describe what you think is a "divinely anointed manner."

MEDITATION

*"Prophecy means the expressed thoughts of God spoken in a language that no man in his natural gift of speech could articulate on his own. The substance and nature of prophecy exceed the limits that the human mind is capable of thinking or imagining. Its purpose is to edify, exhort, and comfort either individuals or the corporate Body of Christ. Although prophecy comes **through** the mouth or pen of man, it comes **from** the mind of God"*

(*The Seer*, Page 19).

Have you ever "heard" God speak in your inner man, speaking things that you could never have articulated on your own? How did you know it was God and not your own mind? Have you ever been able to use God's thoughts to edify, exhort, or comfort others?

DAY *2*

The Seer Realm

FORMERLY IN ISRAEL, WHEN A MAN WENT TO INQUIRE OF GOD, HE USED TO SAY, "COME, AND LET US GO TO THE SEER"; FOR **HE WHO IS CALLED** A PROPHET NOW WAS FORMERLY CALLED A SEER.

(1 SAMUEL 9:9, EMPHASIS ADDED)

Within the overall realm of the prophet lies the particular and distinctive realm of *the seer*....The word *seer* describes a particular type of prophet who receives a particular type of prophetic revelation or impartation. ...

When it comes to prophetic revelation, a prophet is primarily an inspired hearer and then speaker while a seer is primarily visual. In other words, the prophet is the *communicative* dimension and the seer is the *receptive* dimension. Whereas *nabiy'* emphasizes the active work of the prophet in speaking forth a message from God, *ra'ah* and *chozeh* focus on the experience or means by which the prophet "sees or perceives" that message....

All true seers are prophets, but not all prophets are seers. A prophet may have the particular grace to hear and proclaim the word of the Lord and yet not necessarily function as profusely in the revelatory visionary capacity as a seer does. The seer, on the other hand, may move quite remarkably in this visionary dream capacity yet not be as deep in the inspirational audible graces of hearing and speaking. Nevertheless, both move and operate in the prophetic realm, but in different capacities or dimensions.

(Quote From *The Seer*, Pages 21-23)

QUESTIONS

1. The author describes one difference between a prophet and a seer by saying that a prophet hears revelation and speaks it while a seer sees revelation. Have you ever experienced these two types of revelation? Do you know someone who has?

2. Because a seer is a receptive dimension of prophetic revelation and the prophet is the communicative dimension, how does this help explain that all true seers are prophets but not all prophets are seers?

3. What kind of faith does it take for a prophet to speak forth a message from God? What safeguards do you think a prophet should take to be sure the message is really what he or she has heard?

4. When a seer receives a prophetic revelation, how is it received? How does the seer's picture or vision bring God's revelation to others? Does the seer need to always speak what he or she sees?

5. From your experience, comment on seers and prophets and their usefulness in the Body of Christ. What were some immediate reactions to what was shared? Have you seen positive results from what was revealed?

"[The seer realm] of prophetic anointing
has a lot to do with quietly waiting on God.
…Quite often, impartation in the seer realm
comes only after a time of patient waiting
and contemplative meditation upon the Lord.
But thank the Lord, if we wait, He will come!"
(*The Seer*, Page 24).

How much time do you spend waiting on
God during an average day? During an average
week? Is God asking you to increase your time
waiting on Him so that He might impart more to you?

Two Prophetic Streams: Contrasts and Comparisons

[I PRAY] THAT THE GOD OF OUR LORD JESUS CHRIST, THE FATHER OF GLORY, MAY GIVE TO YOU A SPIRIT OF WISDOM AND OF REVELATION IN THE KNOWLEDGE OF HIM. (EPHESIANS 1:17).

By contrasting and comparing the prophet and seer streams, we can gain a better understanding of how the two work together and complement each other in bringing out the fullest expression of God's prophetic revelation. ...

Prophets in this stream often work in a plurality of leadership. Seasoned and gifted individuals, both men and women, minister through the laying on of hands, relating prophecy to individuals or to the corporate body as it is revealed to them. This ministry often utilizes the spiritual gifts of tongues and the interpretation of tongues, prophecy and words of knowledge. A *nabiy'* prophet "hears" a word in their spirit and begins by releasing this unction. This kind of prophecy tends to be more spontaneous and with a faster flow than "seer" prophecy, with inspiration as the general tone.

A *ra'ah* or *chozeh* seer, on the other hand, tends more toward single-person ministry versus the plurality of a team. The seer anointing emphasizes visions and the revelatory gifts mingled with the gift of discerning of spirits rather than the audible, speaking gifts. Within the visionary dimension there are two basic levels of "seeing": *visual* and *actual.*

Visual "seeing" involves insights, revelations, warnings, and prophecies from the Spirit of God that may come in supernatural visual dreams....In contrast, *actual* "seeing" involves supernatural dreams in which God's tangible presence is evident or manifested.

(Quote From *The Seer*, Page 26)

QUESTIONS

1. Have you ever been part of an experience where prophets laid hands on you or someone you know and ministered their revelation? Describe the experience. What was the atmosphere in the "spiritual realm"?

2. Why do you think the ministry of a prophet is usually spontaneous in its flow? Do you think this spontaneity helps keep prophets from adding their own thoughts, or do you think it could make the message more tainted with personal observations?

3. How are the spiritual gifts of tongues, interpretation of tongues, prophecy, and words of knowledge utilized by prophets? How have you seen them operate?

4. Have you experienced the ministry of a seer who spoke of a vision or picture revealed by God? Why does this ministry flow often give the pictures of revelation at a time prior to when they need to be told?

5. How would you explain these basic levels of vision: visual and actual? How do you think these ways of "seeing" work?

MEDITATION

"Every born again believer has two sets of eyes.
We have our physical eyes, with which we view
the physical, created world around us. Paul talks
about a second set of eyes—the eyes of our heart,
or our inner self—that can be enlightened
to perceive spiritual truth....I am convinced that
any believer can develop the seer capacity"

(*The Seer*, Page 28).

Pray that the Lord develops the eyes of
your heart so that you will perceive spiritual truth.

Dimensions of the Prophetic Anointing

FOR THE TESTIMONY OF JESUS IS THE SPIRIT OF PROPHECY.

(REVELATION 19:10B)

Essentially, the anointing is the supernatural enablement or grace—the manifested presence of the Holy Spirit—operating upon or through an individual or a corporate group to produce the works of Jesus. It means God with you and God in you; you are talking His talk and walking in His shadow.

As an anointed people, we as the Body of Christ have been called to carry a prophetic-type burden which will cause us to live on the cutting edge of God's eternal purpose. The prophetic ministry is but one aspect of the fivefold calling of apostles, prophets, evangelists, pastors, and teachers. As such, it is resident to a degree in every ministry, and more evident and active in certain ones. God's ultimate weapon is a man or a woman who has encountered the prophetic anointing. God does not anoint *projects*; He anoints *people*!

Persons anointed with a prophetic ministry speak the word of the Lord in the name of the Lord. They carry weight in the church by virtue of the ethical, moral, and spiritual urgency of their message. Their credentials, credibility, and status as prophetic vessels stem not from birth or by official designation, but by the power of their inner call and by the response of those who hear them.

(Quote From *The Seer*, Pages 32-33)

QUESTIONS

1. If the anointing is supernatural enablement or grace from the Holy Spirit, how does the Spirit determine who receives it? Is it available to all believers? Why or why not?

2. Consider what it means to have a supernatural anointing upon a corporate group. How does this work? Have you experienced corporate anointing? How did it affect the individual participants as well as the entire group?

3. Explain the statement, "God with you and God in you, you are talking His talk and walking in His shadow." How can people tell this is happening to you?

4. What is the "cutting edge of God's eternal purpose"? How can we live there? What part do we play in this type of life?

5. Because the prophetic ministry is resident to a degree in every ministry, determine those ministries in which it is more evident and active. Why?

MEDITATION

*"The single most characteristic mark of a true
prophetic person is the evidence that he or she
has stood in the counsel of God and has, therefore,
faithfully declared what he or she heard from His mouth"*
(The Seer, Page 33).

*Have you stood in the counsel of God? Have
you been faithful to declare what you have heard
from the Lord? If these experiences are new to you
or if your life has been marked by multiple incidents,
you still need to grow further in His presence.
Plan time in your devotional time to wait and listen.
Then follow through when you hear His direction.*

Understanding the Prophetic Anointing

BLESSED ARE THE PURE IN HEART, FOR THEY SHALL SEE GOD.   (MATTHEW 5:8)

Today there is a new anointing for a new generation, a Joshua generation of people who will be born into the things of the Spirit in the midst of a great spiritual storm that is sweeping across our land. Let's take a closer look at this anointing. ...

Usually, prophets make no special claim to be heard but are content to speak and act and leave the matter there, confident not in themselves but in the fact that they have heard from God and that every word from Him will find fulfillment. Their primary concern is not with the distant future but to tell forth the will of God in the crisis of their own days. Prophets, then, are essentially interpreters of God.

The prophecies of the Old Testament prophets foreshadowed Christ. The major task of New Testament prophets and beyond has always been to declare that in Christ all the prophecies of the Bible have been fulfilled. ...

Remember that prophecy itself is the expressed thoughts of God spoken in a language that no man in his natural gift of speech could articulate on his own. The substance and nature of prophecy exceed the limits of what the natural mind could conceive. Prophecy comes *through* the mouth of man but *from* the mind of God—spiritual thoughts in spiritual words.

(Quote From *The Seer*, Pages 32-34)

COMMENTS

Look at the variations of prophetic grace listed below (*The Seer*, Pages 34-43) and make comments in each box

Variation	How God Uses This Area	My Experience in
Dreamers and Visionaries		
Prophets Who Proclaim God's Corporate Purpose		
Prophets Who Proclaim God's Heart Standards for His People		
Prophets Who Proclaim the Church's Social Responsibilities and Actions		
Prophets Who Speak Forth the Administrative Strategy of God With a Political Slant		
Prophetic Worship Leaders Who Usher in the Manifested Presence of God Through Prophetic Worship		
Prophetic Intercessors		
Spirit-Bearers		
Prophetic Counselors		
Prophetic Equippers		
Prophetic Writers		
Prophetic Evangelists		

"The prophetic anointing of the Spirit makes itself known in a wide variety of ways. People are different, with different personalities, cultures, ethnic backgrounds and different gifts....It should not be surprising then, that there is a great divergent expression of the ministry and office of the prophet....These various models represent what the Spirit is doing and desires to do in the church. Together they present a more complete picture of the fullness of the Lord's prophetic anointing"

(*The Seer*, Page 34).

How does your personality, culture, and background bring uniqueness to the expression of your spiritual gifts? How do they present a part of the picture of the fullness of the Lord's prophetic anointing?

Poison and Antidote

NOW, THERE ARE VARIETIES OF GIFTS, BUT THE SAME
SPIRIT. AND THERE ARE VARIETIES OF MINISTRIES, AND THE
SAME LORD. AND THERE ARE VARIETIES OF EFFECTS, BUT
THE SAME GOD WHO WORKS ALL THINGS IN ALL **PERSONS**.

(1 CORINTHIANS 12:4-6, EMPHASIS ADDED)

Clearly...the prophetic anointing manifests in many diverse ways. All arise from the same Holy Spirit, who gives as He wills. With this in mind, a warning is in order. There is a deadly poison that can kill our ministry and our ability to walk in our anointing, whatever it may be: the poison of covetousness. Comparing ourselves to someone else and wanting what they have produces death. We should never judge or evaluate our anointing by someone else's anointing. It is vitally important to avoid jealousy and insecurity. God has plenty of anointing to go around. Let's be satisfied to seek our own calling and walk in our own anointing.

The antidote to this poison is to learn to walk in accountability with others, cultivating faithfulness while giving ourselves to the unique expression of grace that God has imparted to each of us. Sometimes we are prone to allow ourselves to be hindered by rejection, criticism, legalistic traditions, and the restrictive yokes and molds of others' unrealistic and erroneous expectations.

The Holy Spirit will help us and liberate us to be unique and varied expressions of His wonderful prophetic presence and yet walk circumspectly with integrity within the Church.

(Quote From *The Seer*, Page 43)

QUESTIONS

1. When God assembles the people of God, the anointing manifests itself in diverse ways. Why do people often tend to think that there is a formula or one-size-fits-all anointing?

2. Why does covetousness become a major deterrent to the anointing? How does this happen? Have you ever coveted another person's anointing or experience?

3. Have you ever judged or evaluated your gifts or anointing by someone else's anointing? What dangers lie in such an evaluation? How can we be freed from such comparisons?

4. When we are satisfied with our own calling, we acknowledge certain aspects of God's character. What are some of these? How does faith come into play in order to walk in our own anointing?

5. Do you have accountable persons with whom you can cultivate faithfulness to your gifts? If so, how do they call you to accountability? If not, who could become your team of exhorters to keep you on track?

MEDITATION

*"God has never been in a box. We are the ones
in boxes! It is time to let the Holy Spirit take
the lid off so that, in gratitude **to** Him, we can
become all that we can be **in** Him. Let's let His
anointing break the yoke. Instead of wishing we
were somebody else or had what somebody else has,
let's be faithful and accountable to walk in the unique
expression of grace that God has given to each of us"*
(The Seer, Page 44).

*What box are you in? What will you
do to let the Holy Spirit take the lid off your box?*

Vision: The Power That Sustains

WHERE THERE IS NO VISION, THE PEOPLE ARE UNRE-
STRAINED, BUT HAPPY IS HE WHO KEEPS THE LAW.

(PROVERBS 29:18)

This verse in the New International Version reads: "Where there is no *revelation*, the people cast off restraint; but blessed is he who keeps the law" (emphasis added). Some other translations, such as the New Revised Standard Version, use the word "prophecy" instead of "vision" or "revelation." The point is clear: without prophecy, without divine revelation or vision, people will cast off all restraint. They will run wild because they have no guidance—no *vision*. The Word of God—His *law*—provides vision and guidance for living, and those who follow it are blessed.

Everyone needs a vision to sustain them in life…. The apostle Paul set his sights on knowing Christ, which he acknowledged was a lifelong process.

Brethren, I do not regard myself as having laid hold of it yet; but one thing I do: forgetting what lies behind and reaching forward to what lies ahead, I press on toward the goal for the prize of the upward call of God in Christ Jesus. Let us therefore, as many as are perfect, have this attitude (Philippians 3:13-15a).

Like Paul, we need to be a people of vision. Let us set our sights on the Lord and aim at His goals.

(Quote From *The Seer*, Pages 45-47)

QUESTIONS

1. Looking at the different translations of Proverbs 29:18 above, make your own "amplified version" that explains the words of this verse in terms of your life.

2. How does the Word of God provide vision for our lives? Besides the Ten Commandments, where can you find guidance for living? In what ways have you received blessings when you followed the Word?

3. "Everyone needs a vision to sustain them in life." What does this mean for someone who is in the 20-40 year bracket? For those in their 50's and 60's? What about for senior citizens?

4. What do you believe is "lying ahead" (Phil. 3:13-15a) for you in the near future? What has God spoken about your long-term future?

5. How do you set your sights on the Lord when you make major life decisions? How do you ensure that you are aimed at His goals and not merely your own?

*"As Christians, we are called to be a people
of vision. We must learn to set a goal or target in front
of our eyes to gaze upon. It is only when we aim
at something that we have any chance of hitting it!"*
(*The Seer*, Page 47).

*How do your priorities reflect your goal or target?
Is your target easy to aim at? Are you
easily distracted from achieving your goal?*

The Vision That Sustained Zechariah

ON THE TWENTY-FOURTH DAY OF THE ELEVENTH MONTH, WHICH IS THE MONTH OF SHEBAT, IN THE SECOND YEAR OF DARIUS, THE WORD OF THE LORD CAME TO ZECHARIAH THE PROPHET, THE SON OF BERECHIAH, THE SON OF IDDO.... (ZECHARIAH 1:7).

Zechariah was a visionary prophet whose visions related specifically to the time after the Babylonian exile and the beginning of the Messianic period in Israel's history....

In his vision, Zechariah saw an elaborate golden lampstand with two olive trees on either side of it. His first response was very intelligent. He asked the angel, "What are these, my lord?" Asking a question is a wise course of action whenever visionary revelation occurs. That is a lesson I learned from Zechariah. No matter what I see or how many times I think I may have seen it before, I always ask, "What is this, Lord?" I am confident that the same God who gives me the revelation can also interpret it for me.

Even when the angel asks him specifically, "Do you not know what these are?" Zechariah answers with humility, "No, my lord." Had Zechariah not responded with humility and openness, he probably would not have gained much from the whole experience. People who think they know it all already cut themselves off from learning anything new....

This...vision sustained Zechariah...Zerubbabel and all of the returning exiles. It encouraged and motivated them to rebuild the temple in Jerusalem, as well as the walls of the city and the city itself, which had been destroyed by the Babylonians. Vision sustains a people, and humility is a key that releases understanding!

(Quote From *The Seer*, Pages 50-52)

QUESTIONS

1. Have you ever had a vision or revelation that had to do with governmental or social concerns? Why would God give such visions or revelations to nongovernmental or social leaders?

2. When God has spoken or revealed something to you that you did not understand, have you asked questions to receive further clarification? Do you ask your Christian leaders for clarification, when you need it?

3. Humility and openness characterized Zechariah's response to the angel. Why are these two traits important to anyone involved in revelation or visionary gifts?

4. Understanding the message of a revelation or vision is important, but why is it also important to "gain from the experience"? What can be learned through the experience?

5. It must have been exhilarating to Zechariah to see the faith that accompanied the exiles and the leaders as they rebuilt what had once been destroyed. What has been destroyed in your life, community, or church that needs rebuilt? What can stir the faith of those who need to be motivated to make a difference?

*"Zechariah's vision had to do with a message
for Zerubbabel, the civic official of the returning
exiles under whose leadership the temple in
Jerusalem would be rebuilt. The word of the Lord
to Zerubbabel was, 'Not by might nor by power,
but by My Spirit.' This was meant as an
encouragement to Zerubbabel and the rest of the
returning exiles that a new era was beginning, an
era characterized by the working of God's Spirit
in power, and the coming day of the Messiah"*
(*The Seer*, Page 52).

*God spoke to a civic official through an established
prophet. Does God still desire to speak to civic officials
today? Whom might He choose to speak through?*

Seeking the Vision That Sustains Us

[I PRAY] THAT THE EYES OF YOUR HEART MAY BE ENLIGHT-
ENED, SO THAT YOU WILL KNOW WHAT IS THE HOPE OF
HIS CALLING, WHAT ARE THE RICHES OF THE GLORY OF
HIS INHERITANCE IN THE SAINTS, AND WHAT IS THE SUR-
PASSING GREATNESS OF HIS POWER TOWARD US WHO
BELIEVE.   (EPHESIANS 1:18-19)

Keeping our vision of the Lord clear before us will sustain us through the many labors of our life and ministry....

Over the years, I have become convinced that in the Christian life at least two things are certain: God *never* changes, and we are *always* changing. Our life as a Christian is a continual transition from one place to another, one level to another, one understanding to another. The purpose of spiritual light is to bring us into change and growth. The more light we have, the more change we experience, and the more we change (for the better) the more we are brought into higher levels of glory. Unless we are in constant transition, we will stop somewhere along the way and settle down. The Christian life is a frontier. God did not call us to be settlers but to be pilgrims and pioneers. This is the point of Paul's prayer in the first chapter of Ephesians....

The more enlightenment we have, the more wisdom and revelation we are open to receive, and the greater understanding we can develop of the hope of His calling, the glory of His inheritance, and the surpassing greatness of His power as they apply to our lives.

(Quote From *The Seer*, Page 54)

QUESTIONS

1. How has keeping your vision of the Lord clear before you sustained you through your labors in ministry and in your life?

2. How do you personally know that God never changes? What Scripture confirms this to you? What experiences have you had to testify that this is true?

3. How do you know that humanity is always changing? Where do you find this in Scripture? Have you seen this to be true in your experience?

4. How well do you weather transitions in your life? Do you see your transitions as bringing you from one level to the next? Do they help you grow in your understanding?

5. What factors help us develop the understanding of the hope of God's calling and His surpassing greatness? How can we develop these factors?

MEDITATION

"We need a vision to sustain us as a people—a vision that shows us clearly how the promises of God are more than all the power of evil. Let us then be a people of vision who will not perish but walk together in hot pursuit of the Lord, that we too will be able to hold before our eyes an all-consuming vision of the conquering Son of Man and the Ancient of Days sitting upon His throne"
(*The Seer*, Page 54).

Do others have the same vision as you? Are you walking in hot pursuit with others of like vision as you?

The Diversity of Visionary States—Part 1

BUT ONE AND THE SAME SPIRIT WORKS ALL THESE THINGS, DISTRIBUTING TO EACH ONE INDIVIDUALLY JUST AS HE WILLS.   (1 CORINTHIANS 12:11)

There is only one Holy Spirit, but He works in a multiplicity of ways. There are many spiritual gifts, but only one gift-giver: the Holy Spirit of God. The prophetic anointing manifests itself in many diverse ways, but they all derive from the same Spirit....

This same diversity by the one Spirit applies also to visionary states and experiences. In fact, the New Testament uses a variety of Greek words to express different visionary states. None of these states are "higher" or "better" than any of the others. They are simply different, and the Holy Spirit uses them with different people for different purposes.

Let's take a closer look at some of these visionary states....

Onar

In Greek, *onar* is the common word for "dream." It refers simply to the kind of dreaming we all do when we sleep. Everyday dreams are themselves visionary in nature because our minds generate images that we "see" while we are asleep. As the Bible makes clear, God can and does use these common dreams to communicate with ordinary people....

Enupnion

Like *onar*, the word *enupnion* refers to a vision or dream received while asleep. The difference with *enupnion* is that it stresses a surprise quality that is contained in that dream.

(Quote From *The Seer*, Page 57-59)

QUESTIONS

1. Why is it important to know that even though there are diverse spiritual gifts, there is only one Giver of those gifts? How does this bring us to respect the gifts that others have?

2. Look up the word "anointing" in a common dictionary. Then find three Scriptures that use this word. What have you learned about what anointing is? Are there specific ingredients necessary, even if there are various ways it is manifested?

3. Do you have the ability to "sense" or know when the prophetic anointing is ready to manifest itself in you or others? In your experience, what takes place before prophecy is given in a corporate setting?

4. Have you had an *onar*, or has someone whom you know had an *onar*? What makes this visionary state different from "ordinary" dreams?

5. Have you experienced an *enupnion*? Do you know of another who has? Why would God want to give a surprise in a dream?

MEDITATION

*"Sometimes a 'surprise element' is released through
seer encounters. Watch out: ready or not, here He comes!"*
(*The Seer*, Page 60).

*How regular are seer encounters in your life? Do
you take the time to wait and pray to receive visions
and revelation from the Lord? Do you prepare for sleep
by asking the Lord to speak to you while you sleep?
Begin a regimen of preparation for bed that includes
inviting God to bring revelation in the night hours.*

The Diversity of Visionary States—Part 2

BOASTING IS NECESSARY, THOUGH IT IS NOT PROFITABLE; BUT I WILL GO ON TO VISIONS AND REVELATIONS OF THE LORD. (2 CORINTHIANS 12:1)

Here are three more New Testament Greek words that express different visionary states.

Horama

Horama is another general term for vision, meaning "that which is seen." It carries the particular sense of a "spectacle, sight, or appearance." New Testament examples commonly associate this word with *waking visions....*

You can be a candidate for *horama* visions....Just tell the Lord of your desire to be a person who receives the spirit of revelation and sees visions. It is in His Word. It is for today. It is there for the asking!

Horasis

A *horasis* occurs when the Spirit who lives within us looks out through the "windows" of our eyes and allows us to see what He sees. Are we seeing in the natural or in the spiritual? Sometimes it is hard to tell, and sometimes it is *both.* When our spiritual eyes are open, sometimes our natural eyes can see into the spiritual realm. We may see dual images as visionary spiritual pictures are superimposed over the images we are seeing with our physical eyes....

Optasia

Another visionary state found in the New Testament is denoted by the word *optasia*—literally meaning "visuality," or in concrete form, "apparition." *Optasia* has the very specific connotation of self-disclosure or of letting oneself be seen. The word...always [occurs] in the context of someone seeing a divine or spiritual personage.

(Quote From *The Seer*, Pages 60, 62-63)

QUESTIONS

1. Have you ever had a *horama* vision, or do you personally know someone who has had one? What did the vision entail? Why do you think God revealed it? Were there results from its revelation?

2. The author encourages us to ask to receive the spirit of revelation and see visions. Have you done this? Why does this type of revelation "scare" some people? Why should we seek *horama* visions?

3. Have you experienced a *horasis*, or do you know of someone who has experienced one? How do both the natural and spiritual work in this visionary state?

4. What is your understanding of the *optasia* visionary state? Have you or someone you know experienced this? What impact can this visionary state have on one's life?

5. Looking at the three visionary states above, which would you say the Lord needs to develop more in His Body? Why?

MEDITATION

"We all have two sets of eyes: our physical or natural eyes, and the 'eyes' of our heart with which we 'see' into the spiritual realm.... Those are the 'eyes' through which we see and understand spiritual truth. The Bible says that our body is a temple for the Holy Spirit. Every temple has windows and doors. When the Lord comes to dwell in our 'temple,' He likes to be able to look out His 'windows.' Our eyes—physical and spiritual—are the windows to our soul"

(The Seer, Page 62).

How well do your eyes work in seeing what the Lord wants you to see?

The Diversity of Visionary States—Part 3

THEREFORE, PREPARE YOUR MINDS FOR ACTION, KEEP SOBER **IN SPIRIT**, FIX YOUR HOPE COMPLETELY ON THE GRACE TO BE BROUGHT TO YOU AT THE REVELATION OF JESUS CHRIST.   (1 PETER 1:13, EMPHASIS ADDED)

Here are the remaining New Testament Greek words that express different visionary states.

Ekstasis

Ekstasis, from which our English word "ecstasy" is derived…means amazement, astonishment, or a trance. Literally, *ekstasis* means "a displacement of the mind," or "bewilderment." When translated as "trance," *ekstasis* refers to one being caught up in the Spirit so as to receive those revelations that God intends.…

Apokalupsis

With *apokalupsis,* we come to the most frequently used word in the New Testament to describe a visionary state.…*Apokalupsis* literally means "disclosure," an "appearing" or "coming," a "manifestation." It carries specifically the sense of something hidden that has now been uncovered or revealed.…

Egenomehn ehn pneumati

The phrase *egenomehn ehn pneumati* literally means "to *become* in the Spirit," a state in which one could see visions and be informed or spoken directly to by the Spirit of God. Therein lies the secret to how we get revelation.…We do it by first getting in the Spirit. The more we are filled with the Spirit and walk in the Spirit, the more we become one with the Spirit, and the more our eyes will be opened to see in the Spirit. He will give us the perception to look into the spiritual realm.

(Quote From *The Seer,* Pages 64-67)

QUESTIONS

1. Have you ever had an *ekstasis* vision, or do you personally know someone who has had this type of vision? What did the vision entail? Why do you think God revealed it? Were there results from its revelation?

2. Have you experienced an *apokalupsis,* or do you know of someone who has experienced this? How do hidden things become revealed in this vision?

3. What is your understanding of the *egenomehn ehn pneumatic* visionary state? Have you or someone you know experienced this? What impact can this visionary state have on one's life?

4. Looking at the three visionary states above, which would you say the Lord needs to develop more in His Body? Why?

5. The author tells us in order to get revelation, we must first get in the Spirit. What does this mean to you? How does a person become one with the Spirit?

MEDITATION

*"Have you ever had an experience where you suddenly felt like a little light went on inside? You may not necessarily have had an actual vision, but just a sense that something that you did not understand, something that was hidden from you, was now revealed. That is an **apokalupsis** type experience"*
(*The Seer*, Page 66).

If you have experienced this type of vision, how did God use it? If you have not experienced this, how can you prepare yourself to be open to such revelation?

Wisely Judging Revelatory

BUT EXAMINE EVERYTHING **CAREFULLY**; HOLD FAST TO
THAT WHICH IS GOOD.

(1 THESSALONIANS 5:21, EMPHASIS ADDED)

There is only one dependable, unshakable guide through the minefield of supernatural encounters. In a world filled with spiritual voices of the New Age and every other type and description, Christians need to know how to make their way through a spiritual field littered with hidden (and deadly) weapons of the enemy designed to wound or destroy the unwary and the undiscerning.

Entire segments of the Body of Christ have "written off" the supernatural aspects of God's Kingdom and His workings in the Church today because of fears about being deceived and led astray. Others have written it off due to excess, abuse and the bad testimony left behind by lone rangers who are not accountable to anyone in the Body of Christ. The prophetic has been given a bad rap at times, but some of the wound has been self-inflicted. Nonetheless God *does speak* to His people today and He is very capable of preserving us from harm and deception....

Since the Bible is our absolute standard against which we must test *all* spiritual experiences, it should be obvious that we need to know and study God's Word....

God has also ordained that we find safety in our relationship to a Bible-believing fellowship.

(Quote From *The Seer*, Pages 71-72)

QUESTIONS

The following building blocks must be firmly in place before we begin to investigate the principles of testing spiritual experiences (page 73). Soberly estimate your personal status for each question.

1. Am I regularly studying the Scriptures?

2. Am I maintaining a life of prayer?

3. Am I seeking purity, cleansing, and holiness in my life?

4. Am I a worshipful member of a local Christian congregation?

5. Am I committed to a few peer relationships that can speak into my life?

"What would you think if you had a spiritual experience that made your hair stand on end? Would you write it off as absolutely satanic or 'off the wall' because it didn't fit your theological code? Many people would, and do. Supernatural encounters are real. The seer dimension into the spirit world is not something relegated to yesterday—it exists today and is on the rise! The question we must answer is: Do all such revelatory encounters come from the one true God or can there be other sources? How can we tell the source or nature of the spirit beings we encounter? What are the marks of a truly God-initiated encounter or revelatory experience?"

(*The Seer*, Page 71).

Answer these questions and allow God to speak direction as to where you need to go from here.

Sources of Revelation

SON OF MAN, PROPHESY AGAINST THE PROPHETS WHO
ARE FOLLOWING THEIR OWN SPIRIT AND HAVE SEEN
NOTHING. (EZEKIEL 13:2-3)

The Scriptures indicate that spiritual revelation or communication comes from any one of three sources: the Holy Spirit, the human soul, and the realm of evil spirits. The need for discernment in this area is obvious.

The Holy Spirit is the only true source of revelation (see 2 Pet. 1:21). It was the Holy Spirit who "moved" the prophets of the Old Testament and the witnesses of the New Testament. The Greek word for "moved," *phero,* means "to be borne along" or even "to be driven along as a wind" (James Strong, *Strong's Exhaustive Concordance of the Bible,* Peabody, Mass.: Hendrickson Publishers, 1988, *moved,* Greek, #5342).

The human soul is capable of voicing thoughts, ideas, and inspirations out of the unsanctified portion of our emotions (see Ezek. 13:1-6; Jer. 23:16). These human inspirations are not necessarily born of God. As Ezekiel the prophet said, they are prophecies "...out of their own hearts...Woe unto the foolish prophets, that follow their own spirit, and have seen nothing" (Ezek. 13:2-3 KJV).

Evil spirits operate with two characteristics common to their master. They can appear as "angels of light" (or as "good voices"), and they always speak lies because they serve the chief liar and the father of lies, satan.... We need to "test" every source and aspect of the revelation—whether it be a dream, apparition, spoken word, or other type.

(Quote From *The Seer,* Pages 73-74)

QUESTIONS

1. Check yourself with the following questions in THE SELF TEST (*The Seer,* Pages 74-75).

    a. Is there any evidence of influences other than the Spirit of God in my life?

    b. What is the essence of the "vision" or revelation? (How does it compare to God's written Word?)

    c. Was I under the control of the Holy Spirit when I received the vision?

        i). Have I presented my life to Jesus Christ as a living sacrifice?

        ii). Have I been obedient to His Word?

        iii). Am I being enlightened with His inspiration?

        iv). Am I committed to doing His will no matter what it is?

        v). Am I yielding my life to the praises of God or to critical speech?

        vi). Am I waiting quietly and expectantly before Him?

2. Understand THE SOURCE TEST (*The Seer,* Pages 75-76).

    a. Have I cut off all pictures put before my mind's eye by satan using the blood of Jesus?

    b. Have I presented the eyes of my heart to the Lord for Him to fill?

    c. Has the Holy Spirit projected on the inner screen of my heart the flow of vision that He desires?

NINE SCRIPTURAL TESTS

(The Seer, Pages 76-78):

1.   *Does the revelation edify, exhort, or console?*

2.   *Is it in agreement with God's Word?*

3.   *Does it exalt Jesus Christ?*

4.   *Does it have good fruit?*

5.   *If it predicts a future event, does it come to pass?*

6.   *Does the prophetic prediction turn people toward God or away from Him?*

7.   *Does it produce liberty or bondage?*

8.   *Does it produce life or death?*

9.   *Does the Holy Spirit bear witness that it is true?*

Look at a recent revelation you have either received or witnessed. Go through each test and evaluate the revelation based on these nine.
What have you learned doing this exercise?

Fifteen Wisdom Issues

BELOVED, DO NOT BELIEVE EVERY SPIRIT, BUT TEST THE SPIRITS TO SEE WHETHER THEY ARE FROM GOD, BECAUSE MANY FALSE PROPHETS HAVE GONE OUT INTO THE WORLD. (1 JOHN 4:1)

The 15 "wisdom issues" listed below…will help us learn how to wisely judge the various forms of revelation we will encounter in our adventure with Christ.

1. *Search for proper exegesis and scriptural context.*

2. *Focus on Jesus.*

3. *Major on the "main and plain" things.*

4. *Follow biblical principles—not the rigid letter of the law.*

5. *Build bridges….We must…keep ourselves clean from spiritual pride.*

6. *Honor and pray for leaders.*

7. *Be aware of times and seasons.*…We can predetermine by His guidance…but also…welcome spontaneous occurrences.

8. *Let love rule.*

9. *Maintain balance.*…There is a godly tightrope of dynamic tension between the reality of subjective experience and biblical doctrine.

10. *Understand the relationship of divine initiation and human response.*…Although some…external, visible, and audible signs are divinely initiated…some of them are human responses and reactions to the Holy Spirit.

11. *Be known by your fruits.*

12. *Perceive the works of God and the motives of man.*

13. *Control your flesh and cooperate with God.*

14. *Be alert and aware.* Let us search Scripture, review Church history, seek the Lord, and receive input from those who are wiser and more experienced than we.

15. *Avoid spiritual ditches.* There are two deep ditches we should avoid. First, we should watch out for *analytical skepticism*…and *fear* (of man, rejection, fanaticism, etc.).

(Quote From *The Seer*, Pages 80-84)

QUESTIONS

1. Looking over the 15 items above, evaluate where you currently stand in each one.

2. How does your personality affect the rating of the wisdom items above?

3. Pick three of the wisdom issues that you have rated highest in your life. How will you help transfer these to someone else? How can you formally or informally mentor them?

4. Look at the three wisdom issues that you rated the lowest. What will you do to bring them forward?

5. Do you see any of these wisdom issues as more important than the others? Why or why not?

"If you can't jump in the middle of it, bless it. If you can't bless it, then patiently observe it. If you can't patiently observe it, then just don't criticize it! Do not stretch out the rod of your tongue against those things you do not understand!"
(*The Seer*, Page 84).

What does this mean to you?

Discerning of Spirits

BUT SOLID FOOD IS FOR THE MATURE, WHO BECAUSE OF
PRACTICE HAVE THEIR SENSES TRAINED TO DISCERN GOOD
AND EVIL.   (HEBREWS 5:14)

Let me clarify that we are talking about two overlapping but different issues here: general discernment, which is a product of experience, discipline, and study, and discerning of spirits, which is a spiritual gift imparted by the Holy Spirit....

Discernment or distinguishing of spirits is different because it goes beyond our natural learning abilities. It is a supernatural gift from the Lord; we cannot earn it. No amount of human insight or learning will enable us to discern between spirits. Only God can impart that ability, and He does so by His sovereign choice. General discernment and the discerning of spirits are different, but related....The principles for growing in both arenas are the same, however: regular meditation on the Word of God, and the crucible of life experience....

Discerning of spirits is the supernatural ability to recognize and distinguish between not only good and bad, but various classes of spirits:

- The Holy Spirit
- Good angels
- Fallen angels
- Demons or evil spirits
- The human spirit

... Sometimes when dealing with the spiritual realm, we can find ourselves facing "gray" areas where things are unclear. That is one time when we need the gift of discerning of spirits to clear away the gray and separate matters into black and white.

(Quote From *The Seer*, Pages 85-87)

1. How would you rate your level of general discernment? What experiences, discipline, and/or study have helped shape your general discernment?

2. How is discerning of spirits different from general discernment? Why is the Holy Spirit needed to impart this gift?

3. If general discernment and discerning of spirits are different, why are the principles for growing in both arenas the same? What are these principles? Are these principles effective in your life?

4. From your understanding, explain the various classes of spirits listed above. Have you been able to distinguish these classes? How can you grow in your awareness of these?

5. What "gray" areas have you had to contend with when discerning spirits? What can help you distinguish between spirits?

*"Basically, discernment is perception, which can come
in a variety of ways. Sometimes it is as simple as an
inner knowledge, a 'gut feeling,' that we cannot explain
yet somehow know is real. This kind of spiritual perception
is often so subtle that we can easily miss it or attribute
it to something else, such as a 'hunch' "*
(*The Seer*, Page 88).

*Have you had "hunches" that turned out to
really be spiritual discernment? Have you thought
you had spiritual discernment in something, when in
actuality it was your own "hunch"? Think about
how you will be able to tell the difference in the future.*

Discerning of the Holy Spirit, of Angels, of Human Spirits, and of Evil Spirits

AND THEY WERE ALL FILLED WITH THE HOLY SPIRIT AND BEGAN TO SPEAK WITH OTHER TONGUES, AS THE SPIRIT WAS GIVING THEM UTTERANCE.

(ACTS 2:4)

When the Spirit came on that Day of Pentecost, He appeared in two forms: wind and fire. There is no indication that these believers knew beforehand *how* the Spirit would appear, but when He came, they knew He was there. Once again, only the gift of discernment could impart this knowledge....

Another area of discernment is the ability to discern the human spirit—the true character or motive behind a person's words or actions—even if hidden from casual view. Jesus possessed this ability to an exceptional degree....No one can "see" faith. We can observe faith in action as it is demonstrated, but only the Spirit of God can impart the ability to discern faith in another....

One area of discernment where we must exercise care, caution, and maturity is in the discerning of evil spirits....Have you ever been in a place or situation where you simply felt the presence of evil? What about a time...where a rotten or unpleasant odor was present with no identifiable natural source? ...

Some of the common "symptoms" of the possible presence of evil spirits in a place are an oppressive atmosphere, a sense of confusion, a pervading sense of loneliness or sadness, a feeling of pressure, and depression. These are just a few examples; there are many more.

(Quote from *The Seer*, Pages 90, 92-95)

1. Why do you think the Spirit appeared in two forms on the Day of Pentecost? What were these and what symbolism do you see in them?

2. What causes you to believe that the disciples used discernment to know the Holy Spirit had come and did not think it was merely an unusual work of nature? How is this type of discernment useful to the Church?

3. How is the ability to discern the human spirit useful to you as a believer? How can you develop this gift?

4. Why do you need to exercise care, caution, and maturity when discerning evil spirits? Do we need to be afraid of these spirits? Explain your answer.

5. Look at the list of "symptoms" of the possible presence of evil spirits above. Have you ever seen these symptoms and received the revelation that they were due to an evil spirit? How can you be sensitized to this possibility in a greater dimension?

*"Not every illness…[is] caused by an evil spirit,
but…we find some people today who are not healed
immediately through prayer or laying on of hands.
In some of these cases, a spirit of infirmity may be
at work, which must be taken care of before healing
will occur. In a visionary sense, such a spirit may be
revealed as appearing like a leech on a person, sucking
the strength out of whatever part of the body is afflicted"*
(*The Seer*, Page 94).

*As graphic as this is, have you ever seen such a vision
of someone? Why would God use such a graphic picture?*

The Purpose of the Gift of Discernment

THE WIND BLOWS WHERE IT WISHES AND YOU HEAR THE
SOUND OF IT, BUT DO NOT KNOW WHERE IT COMES
FROM AND WHERE IT IS GOING; SO IS EVERYONE WHO IS
BORN OF THE SPIRIT.   (JOHN 3:8)

God never gives gifts or imparts spiritual abilities for no reason. Why is the gift of discernment, and the discerning of spirits in particular, so important? There is a sixfold purpose for this gift in the life of the Church:

1. Deliverance from demons. Demons must be discerned and exposed before they can be dealt with....The New Testament contains numerous other accounts of demon-possessed people being delivered by Jesus or His followers. This ministry is essential today....

2. Reveal the servants of satan. Once, when Paul was sharing the Word of God with a Roman proconsul, he was opposed by a magician named Elymas (see Acts 13:8-12).

3. Expose and defeat the work and utterance of demons. This is clearly illustrated in Acts 16:16-18 when Paul casts the spirit of divination out of the slave girl....

4. Expose error. Discerning of spirits reveals not only the workers of satan, but the errors of their teachings as well....

5. Acknowledge and confess Christ....As the spirit of prophecy is poured out, people will fall on their face and declare that Jesus is Lord (1 Cor. 14:24-25).

6. Know the moving of the Holy Spirit so as to cooperate with Him....Unless we recognize (discern) where and how the Holy Spirit is moving, we could find ourselves unintentionally working at cross-purposes to Him.

(Quote from *The Seer*, Page 95)

1. The author tells us, "God never gives gifts or imparts spiritual abilities for no reason." What does this mean to you? Has your life experience borne this out?

2. Explain why the gift of discernment and the discerning of spirits are so important. Has this been true in your life? How do these gifts help us in life decisions?

3. Look at the six purposes for the gift of discernment and the gift of discerning of spirits in the life of the Church. Think through the experiences you have in each one. Which purpose has been most demonstrated in your life thus far?

4. Of these six purposes, which seems to be the most important to you at this time? Why?

5. How do these purposes help express the desires of God for the Church to be wise? How do these purposes demonstrate the effectual work of the Holy Spirit to train us?

MEDITATION

*"The operation of the Holy Spirit is especially needed
in 'religious' cities. God have mercy on us and deliver
us from the slumbering effects of religious spirits.
Where the Spirit of the Lord is, there is freedom!"*
(The Seer, Page 96).

*Is the city or town you live in "religious"? How do
you need to pray for your city so that it would receive the
Spirit of the Lord and the freedom that accompanies Him?*

Guidelines for Operating in the Gift of Discernment

BY THIS YOU KNOW THE SPIRIT OF GOD: EVERY SPIRIT THAT CONFESSES THAT JESUS CHRIST HAS COME IN THE FLESH IS FROM GOD. (1 JOHN 4:2)

I want to share six guidelines for walking uprightly and effectively in that gift.

1. Cultivate the gift. We can cultivate the gift of discernment by regularly exercising our spiritual senses, learning to give a spiritual interpretation of what our normal senses perceive during a visionary experience....

2. Test the spirits. Don't automatically assume that every vision or spiritual presence is from God. He commands us to test the spirits in order to distinguish the true from the false....

3. Examine the fruit. One of the best ways to test the spirits is to look at the results, keeping in mind that fruit takes time to develop....

4. Discerning of spirits is *not* the gift of suspicion. It is easy to fall into the trap of using this gift to "see" things about other people and "report" what we see in a way that hurts or damages them....

5. Wisdom, wisdom, wisdom! Wisdom is an *absolute* necessity in exercising the gift of discernment....Such wisdom comes only from God.

6. Intercede! Along with the gift of discernment may come faith to act or pray with authority....The key, however, is to *always* pray first for discernment so that we will know what to do in any specific situation.

(Quote From *The Seer*, Page 97)

1. How do you cultivate your gift of discernment? How do you exercise your spiritual senses?

2. In what ways do you test the spirits? Are you easily able to distinguish between what is true and what is false?

3. How thoroughly do you examine the fruit of those who are prophets in today's world? Why are younger prophets under more scrutiny than those who have been in ministry a long time?

4. Explain the difference between *suspicion* and *discernment*. Have you been able to avoid suspicion? Are you able to discern without judgment?

5. Why is wisdom so important when using the gift of discernment? How do we get wisdom? Do you spend time with the Lord so that you receive all the wisdom you need? Explain.

MEDITATION

"The gift of distinguishing of spirits is needed today.
Deliverance is needed today. Supernatural strength
and aid are needed today! Though the term "seer" is
used in the Old Testament, technically, it is not used
in the New. It is my view that the gift of discerning
of spirits encompasses these seer perceptive capacities.
Let's call them forth and welcome them for
the edifying of the Body of Christ"
(*The Seer*, Page 98).

Take time to pray, calling these gifts
forth first in yourself and in your church.

Dream Language

IF THERE IS A PROPHET AMONG YOU, I, THE LORD, SHALL MAKE MYSELF KNOWN TO HIM IN A VISION. I SHALL SPEAK WITH HIM IN A DREAM. (NUMBERS 12:6B)

The Lord spoke these words to Miriam and Aaron when they challenged Moses' position as God's sole spokesman to the Israelites. He went on to say that His relationship with Moses was different, because He spoke to Moses face to face or, literally, "mouth to mouth" (Num. 12:8). For our purpose, the pertinent point is that God clearly states here that dreams and visions are avenues He will use to speak to His prophets—in the past, the present, and the future.

While dreams are a specific portion of the prophetic ministry, they are not limited only to the prophetically gifted. Joel 2:28 says, "It will come about after this that I will pour out My Spirit on all mankind; and your sons and daughters will prophesy, your old men will dream dreams, your young men will see visions." This Scripture was fulfilled on the Day of Pentecost and continues to be fulfilled in our own day. It is time for the Church to return to a biblical understanding of dreams as an avenue of discerning God's voice.

Dreams are closely associated with visions. The primary difference is that dreams occur during the hours of sleep, while visions usually take place while one is fully awake or conscious. Both means of visual revelation have solid biblical precedent.

(Quote From *The Seer,* Page 101)

Look at the following examples when God spoke to heathens through dreams (*The Seer*, Pages 102-104). Complete the following chart.

Person	Scripture	Important Aspects of Dream Result	Result
Abimelech	Gen. 20		
Laban	Gen. 31		
Midianite soldier	Judg. 7		
Pharaoh's butler and baker	Gen. 40		
Pharaoh	Gen. 41		
Nebuchadnezzar	Dan. 2		
The wise men	Matt. 2		
Pilate's wife	Matt. 27		

"May the Lord raise up men and women
of revelation and excellence once again to give
the timely counsel of God to those in authority"
(*The Seer*, Page 104).

Take time to pray that God would do this in your life,
the life of your local church, and the Church at large.

The Symbolic Language of Dreams

AND IT WILL COME ABOUT AFTER THIS THAT I WILL POUR
OUT MY SPIRIT ON ALL MANKIND; AND YOUR SONS AND
DAUGHTERS WILL PROPHESY, YOUR OLD MEN WILL DREAM
DREAMS, YOUR YOUNG MEN WILL SEE VISIONS.

(JOEL 2:28)

Dreams are the language of emotions and often contain much symbolism....Generally speaking, biblical symbols can be classified into seven different categories:

1. Symbolic actions. In Ephesians 2:6...two symbolic actions—raising and seating—describe what God has done for us spiritually through Christ....

2. Symbolic colors. In prophetic dreams, specific colors often symbolize specific things....

3. Symbolic creatures....In Rev. 12:9, two symbolic creatures— the dragon and the serpent—are used to represent satan....

4. Symbolic directions. For example, "up" often means toward God or toward righteousness, while "down" means the opposite....

5. Symbolic names. One common characteristic of names in the Bible is that they often reflect the character of the individual....Names carry weight in the spirit. Often their meaning is more than just symbolic.

6. Symbolic numbers. Numbers have great symbolic meaning throughout the Bible. Man was created on the sixth day and God finished His work and rested on the seventh. The introduction and the interpretation of these numbers are consistent throughout Scripture....

7. Symbolic objects....A rock as a symbol for the Lord is quite common in the Bible (see Ps. 18:2 and 1 Cor. 10:4). Many other common objects are used in a similar way, such as shields, bowls, harps, candlesticks, etc.

(Quote From *The Seer*, Pages 105-106)

QUESTIONS

Looking at the experiences you have had thus far in dreams and visions, fill out the chart below:

Symbol	What You Know	What You Would Like to Learn
Actions		
Colors		
Creatures		
Directions		
Names		
Numbers		
Objects		

MEDITATION

*"One important point to remember in trying
to understand dream language is that God is
consistent with His symbolic language. How He
speaks in Genesis is similar to how He speaks in
Revelation. Throughout the Bible, the types and
symbols remain very much the same. This same consistency
of symbolism holds true in our own lives as well"*
(*The Seer*, Page 105).

*Can you see the use of symbolism in your dream
language? Ask the Lord to give you the knowledge
to interpret symbols that He can use to guide you.*

Wisdom Points to Remember

IF A PROPHET OR A DREAMER OF DREAMS ARISES AMONG YOU AND GIVES YOU A SIGN OR A WONDER, AND THE SIGN OR THE WONDER COMES TRUE, CONCERNING WHICH HE SPOKE TO YOU, SAYING, "LET US GO AFTER OTHER GODS (WHOM YOU HAVE NOT KNOWN) AND LET US SERVE THEM," YOU SHALL NOT LISTEN TO THE WORDS OF THAT PROPHET OR THAT DREAMER OF DREAMS; FOR THE LORD YOUR GOD IS TESTING YOU TO FIND OUT IF YOU LOVE THE LORD YOUR GOD WITH ALL YOUR HEART AND WITH ALL YOUR SOUL. (DEUTERONOMY 13:1-3)

Dreams and visions can be exciting and wonderful as a means of receiving insight and revelation as long as they come from the right source. Remember that dreams and visions can arise from three places: the demonic realm, the soulish realm (our own human mind and spirit) and the Holy Spirit. In order to be effective either giving or receiving visionary revelation, we must be able to distinguish the source. This is where the gift and discipline of discernment is so important.

Another important factor is giving careful attention to our environment. There may be occasions, for example, when we will have to remove from our homes some things that should not be there, such as certain cultic, occultic, or even soulish-tie objects, before our sleep will be sweet and clean and our environment ready to receive pure revelation. We must be careful to identify and close off all potential demonic entrances to our home in Jesus' name....

Dreams and visions are wonderful, but our life is more than just dreams and visions. Our life is in our Master, Jesus Christ. Someone may reveal true and accurate information and still be a deceptive tool of the enemy to seduce us and draw us in by fascination, and lead us away from Christ.

(Quote From *The Seer*, Pages 111-112)

1. What have you learned about understanding the source of revelation as it comes to your life? Of the three sources of revelation, what tools do you have to distinguish between them?

2. How does the discipline of discernment work in your life at present? How would you like to grow in this discipline? What will be your first steps to do so?

3. Have you looked throughout your house to be sure there are no objects that represent cults or occults? If not, plan to do so. What can "cleaning" these things out of your home do for you and your family?

4. What are soul-tie objects? How do you identify them? Have you taken time to rid your home of these? If not, plan a time when you will.

5. How can someone "reveal true and accurate information and still be a deceptive tool of the enemy to seduce us..."? Have you experienced such a deception? How can you identify such a person?

"Don't simply get caught up in the glitter and glamour of revelatory seers. Examine their message. Look at their lifestyle. What is their conduct? What actions is he or she calling for? If they call for something that is contrary to the principles found in the written Word of God, then they are deceived, immature at best, or even a false prophet, no matter how genuine their visions seem to be or how powerful the message" (*The Seer*, Pages 112-113).

Think about these cautions, and pray these into your life so that you will have wisdom in terms of revelatory gifts.

Levels of Supernatural Visions

I SPEAK THE THINGS WHICH I HAVE SEEN WITH MY FATHER. (JOHN 8:38A)

How do visions "happen"? …

A mental "snapshot" is a good way to describe how visions can happen. Think of how an instant camera works. The shutter opens, allowing light to enter through the lens, imprinting on the film the image that is in front of the lens. The film develops "instantly" so the image can be viewed and analyzed. In a vision, "light" from the Lord enters the "lens" of our spiritual eyes and imprints an image on the "film" of our heart and our mind. As the image "develops," we gain a better understanding of what it means. Most visions are internal in nature. An image is ingrained in our memory, and we can take it out, look at it, and study it any time we need.

Another way to understand how visions happen is to think of each believer in Christ as a house or temple. First Corinthians 6:19 says that our bodies are temples of the Holy Spirit.…Houses generally have windows that let in light. Our eyes are the windows of our soul. Sometimes Jesus, who lives in our house, likes to look out of His windows and share with us what He sees. That is when a vision occurs—we see what Jesus sees when He looks out the windows of His house.

(Quote From *The Seer*, Page 115)

QUESTIONS

1. Have you had a vision? Does the camera analogy fit for the visions you have either had or ones you have heard about? Explain.

2. "An image is ingrained in our memory, and we can take it out, look at it, and study it any time we need." How does this boost the usefulness of a vision?

3. As a house or temple of the Holy Spirit, how do your eyes provide "windows" to your soul? What have they seen that has helped you in your life?

4. Is the concept new to you that Jesus looks out the windows of your soul and shares with you what He sees? What does this say about keeping our windows clean and clear?

5. How would you evaluate the average Christian's experience with visions? What needs to be done to help encourage visions in mature believers?

MEDITATION

"Jesus walked by faith and always pleased His
Father (see John 8:29). He discerned (saw) His
Father's acts and acted accordingly....It seems that
in the life of Jesus, His spiritual eye perceived things
that His mind did not always visualize. Such spiritual
perceptions could be the operation of the gift of a word
of wisdom, word of knowledge, discerning of spirits,
the gift of faith or even the gift of prophecy. Often, the
higher the level of spiritual vision, the higher the dimension
of spiritual sight occurs. I, like you, want to follow Jesus'
example and 'do what we see the Father doing' "

(*The Seer*, Page 116).

How much do you walk by faith like Jesus did?
Do you reflect His ability to perceive what His Father
was doing both by His spiritual eye and His mind?
How can you become more like Him in these areas?

Visions, Dreams, and Messages

IF THERE IS A PROPHET AMONG YOU, I, THE LORD, SHALL MAKE MYSELF KNOWN TO HIM IN A VISION. I SHALL SPEAK WITH HIM IN A DREAM. (NUMBERS 12:6B)

The following are brief descriptions of different ways we receive messages.

A **pictorial vision** [is] an image...revealed and can be identified and described in terms of pictures. They are Holy Spirit visual aids! Symbols may or may not be involved....

A **panoramic vision** is one in which a person sees a pictorial vision, not in snapshot form, but in motion in his or her mind....

A **dream** is a visionary revelation from the Holy Spirit that one receives while asleep. Supernatural dreams can occur in any level of sleep: light rest, regular sleep, deep sleep, or even in a trance state....

Audible messages in the spiritual realm can involve people speaking words, or objects making sounds. We can perceive such messages inside of us by our inner ears, or outside of us by our physical ears....

An **appearance or apparition** is different from a pictorial vision in that it is an actual—perhaps tangible and audible—visitation occurring outside of the person....

More than just a spiritual vision, a **divine sight** is an actual disclosing of a supernatural event. It is like an appearance or apparition in that it is an actual occurrence outside of the person or persons experiencing it...[but it] is not of a being but an object or activity.

(Quote From *The Seer*, Pages 117-122)

Use the following chart to check your understanding of the different ways we receive messages (*The Seer*, Pages 117-122).

Method	Your Definition	Your Experience
Pictorial vision		
Panoramic vision		
Dream		
Audible messages		
Appearance or Apparition		
Divine sight		

MEDITATION

"God is not the author of doubt, confusion, or fear.
When God releases His message to us, even through
one of His angels, we should sense purity and holiness,
a reverence to the Lord, and openness, because they have
nothing to hide. The Spirit of God is not afraid to be
tested. We should never fear offending God by testing
the spirits. On the contrary, God is honored when we do
because He told us in His Word to do so (1 John 4:1-3)"
(*The Seer*, Page 120).

Do you have doubts, confusion, or fears about
messages you have received? How do you test the spirits?

Open Heaven

Now it came about in the thirtieth year, on the fifth day of the fourth month, while I was by the river Chebar among the exiles, the heavens were opened and I saw visions of God.   (Ezekiel 1:1)

An "open heaven" is a vision where a hole seems to appear in the immediate sky, the celestial realm is disclosed and heavenly sights of God become seeable. The term "open heaven" originated in historic revivals to describe those times when the manifested presence of God seems to come down in a tangible manner as conviction of sin, conversions, and healings take place. We are now moving from an era of prophetic renewal into a new epoch of the Holy Spirit. We are crossing a threshold into a period of apostolic open heavens for whole cities and regions to be visited by the presence of the Almighty.

Examples of an open heaven are found throughout Scripture. Here are four instances:

- Ezekiel states that "the heavens were opened." He then describes a great cloud sent by God to protect Ezekiel from His brightness. Then he sees flashing lightning, brilliant light, angels, and other details—Ezek. 1:1-4.

- At Jesus' baptism, the "heavens were opened" and the Holy Spirit descended upon Him in the form of a dove. Then the Father spoke audibly...—Matt. 3:16-17.

- As Stephen was being stoned for preaching the gospel, he looked up into Heaven and saw "the sky loosened and the clouds rolled back" and Jesus standing to receive him—Acts 7:55-56.

- The apostle John...while meditating on the Lord's day...hears a voice and sees "a door opened in heaven." He is then shown the One who sits upon the throne and receives many detailed messages from the Lord.

(Quote From *The Seer*, Pages 122-123)

QUESTIONS

1. Does an "open heaven" seem to be a common occurrence or one that is rare? Explain your answer.

2. The results of an open heaven are tangible. What are some of these? Why are tangible results like these important for the legitimacy of the vision?

3. At Jesus' baptism, what were the tangible results of the open heaven?

4. When Stephen was being stoned, what tangible results might have occurred?

5. With the one-of-a-kind revelation that John received when the door opened in heaven, what tangible results have come about?

"[There are] examples of humble authentic vessels in our day who are receiving open heavens and other levels of revelatory activity in their lives. These experiences are on the increase. As the "last days" unfold such encounters will only multiply!"
(*The Seer*, Page 123).

Is this true in your experience? Why or why not?

Heavenly Visitation

I KNOW A MAN IN CHRIST WHO FOURTEEN YEARS AGO—
WHETHER IN THE BODY I DO NOT KNOW, OR OUT OF THE
BODY I DO NOT KNOW, GOD KNOWS—SUCH A MAN WAS
CAUGHT UP TO THE THIRD HEAVEN.

(2 CORINTHIANS 12:2)

The Bible refers to three heavens:

1. The lowest heaven, the atmospheric sky which encircles the earth—Matt. 16:1-3.

2. The second heaven, the stellar heaven that is called outer space, where the sun, moon, stars, and planets reside—Gen. 1:16-17.

3. The third heaven, which is the highest one, and the center around which all realms revolve, is Paradise, the abode of God and His angels and saints—Ps. 11:4.

A heavenly visitation is like an out-of-body experience except that the person's spirit leaves the earth realm, passes through the second heaven, and goes to the third heaven. This can occur while the person is praying, while in a trance or a deep sleep from the Lord, or at death....

In the same way that a person can visit the third heaven by having an out-of-body experience, he or she can also visit the various regions of hell. If he is a sinner, he approaches hell by descending—in death or a near-death experience or in a supernatural vision—and is shown where he is destined to spend eternity unless he repents and accepts Jesus Christ as his personal Lord and Savior. Then he is brought back to earth into his body by the mercy of God.

(Quote From *The Seer*, Pages 127-128)

QUESTIONS

1. There are three Scriptures listed as references for each of the three heavens. Research these in your Bible and note the distinctions. Use a concordance and find other references as well.

2. Have you ever had a heavenly visitation? Do you know someone who has? Read Second Corinthians 12 about Paul's experience. What was the message to Paul? What were the results to his way of thinking? How did he use the experience to teach the Corinthian church?

3. Have you heard or read of people, both Christian and non-Christian, who have had near-death experiences that allowed them to see Heaven or hell? How does God want to use these experiences for them personally? Is there a message beyond the person who has experienced it? If so, what?

4. Does God mean to frighten non-Christians by allowing them to visit hell? Why does He use this type of experience?

5. Why would God allow Christians to visit hell? How might He use such an experience in the life of a believer?

"I believe heavenly visitations have occurred not only in the Bible, but throughout history, and that such experiences will increase as true apostolic ministry emerges in these last days. Join me and express your desire that you might step into all that our Father God has prepared for you"
(*The Seer*, Page 128).

Take some time to tell God your desire to move into everything He has prepared for you.

The Ecstatic
Realms of the Spirit

On the next day, as they were on their way and approaching the city, Peter went up on the house-top about the sixth hour to pray. But he became hungry and was desiring to eat; but while they were making preparations, he fell into a trance.

(Acts 10:9-10)

I decided to study the subject in depth and spend time around godly people who had a lot more experience with [trances and out-of-body experiences] than I did. What I learned is that these kinds of phenomena originated with God; satan merely usurped and corrupted them as he did everything else. *When properly understood and when initiated by the Spirit of God, a trance is an exciting, fabulous, wonderful thing, another powerful visionary experience that brings a person into the heavenly realm.* The *key* is that such an experience *must* be initiated by the Holy Spirit *only*. It must *never* be self-induced.

A trance brings us into the "ecstatic" realm of the Spirit.... Literally, an ecstatic trance is a displacement of the mind; bewilderment that is commonly accompanied by amazement or astonishment. It is a distraction, especially one resulting from great religious fervor and which often includes feelings of great joy, rapture, and delight that arrest the whole mind.

Ekstasis refers to "any displacement, and especially, with reference to the mind, of that alteration of the normal condition by which the person is thrown into a state of surprise or fear or both; or again, in which a person is so transported out of his natural state that he falls into a trance" (W.E. Vine, Merrill F. Unger, William White, Jr., *Vine's Complete Expository Dictionary of Old and New Testament Words*, Nashville, Tenn.: Thomas Nelson Publishers, 1996, New Testament section, p. 24).

(Quote From *The Seer*, Page 129)

QUESTIONS

1. Have you experienced trances or out-of-body experiences? Do you personally know someone who has? If you know of someone, take time to talk with them about their experiences and the effect they have had on their life.

2. How has satan corrupted trances and out-of-body experiences from what you have seen and heard of them? What important criteria ensures us as to whether the ecstatic experience is from God or not?

3. The author describes the ecstatic realm of a trance as "a displacement of the mind." What do you think this means? Why would God want us to experience this?

4. If a trance often results from great religious fervor, why would God want to distract us and bring us into the "feelings of great joy, rapture, and delight"? Why would He want to "arrest the whole mind"?

5. What is your opinion of the ecstatic realm of the Spirit as you understand it thus far? Does fear or excitement characterize your answer? What might you do to understand this dimension to a greater level?

MEDITATION

"[In a trance,] one can be shocked, amazed,
and joyfully 'caught up' in one's emotions due to the
wondrous activity of the Holy Spirit. In a higher level of
trance, one's natural bodily functions are temporarily 'put
on pause,' and the person is caught up in the Spirit (whether
in the body or out of the body is not the primary issue), and
sees, hears, feels, tastes, touches, or even smells the presence of
the Lord in an 'otherworldly' or heavenly sort of way"

(*The Seer*, Page 130).

Does this sound like something you would
like to experience to a greater degree than you have
thus far? If so, plan time with the Lord regularly
where you do not have to hurry but can linger
to receive more of His ecstatic experiences.

Caught Up in the Spirit

AFTER THESE THINGS I LOOKED, AND BEHOLD, A DOOR STANDING OPEN IN HEAVEN, AND THE FIRST VOICE WHICH I HAD HEARD, LIKE THE SOUND OF A TRUMPET SPEAKING WITH ME, SAID, "COME UP HERE, AND I WILL SHOW YOU WHAT MUST TAKE PLACE AFTER THESE THINGS." IMMEDIATELY I WAS IN THE SPIRIT; AND BEHOLD, A THRONE WAS STANDING IN HEAVEN, AND ONE SITTING ON THE THRONE. (REVELATION 4:1-2)

The Bible...contains numerous instances of people undergoing possible trance-like experiences even though the words "trance" or *ekstasis* are not used....

The prophet Ezekiel described many of his visionary experiences as being "lifted up" by the Spirit, which can also describe a trance-like condition:

- "The Spirit lifted me up and took me away..." (Ezek. 3:14).

- "...the Spirit lifted me up between earth and heaven and brought me in the visions of God to Jerusalem..." (Ezek. 8:3).

- "And the Spirit lifted me up and brought me in a vision by the Spirit of God to the exiles in Chaldea" (Ezek. 11:24).

- "And the Spirit lifted me up and brought me into the inner court; and behold, the glory of the Lord filled the house" (Ezek. 43:5)....

It is important to note here that one does not have to be in a trance to "be in the Spirit." However, one who has experienced a trance may be properly said to have been "in the Spirit." ...

God does nothing without a purpose. His purpose in imparting visionary revelation, whether through a trance or any other means, is not just to give us an "experience," but that we might see and know *Him*.

(Quote From *The Seer*, Pages 133-135)

1. Using the four examples from Ezekiel, read the texts surrounding the verses and fill in the chart below.

Scripture Reference	Setting or Situation Ezekiel Was In When He Received the Vision	Main Points of the Vision
Ezekiel 3:14		
Ezekiel 8:3		
Ezekiel 11:24		
Ezekiel 43:5		

2. From the information in your chart, draw conclusions as to why God spoke to Ezekiel using this method. Are there situations in your life where you could use a vision to give you direction or information to move forward?

3. What does it mean to "be in the Spirit"? Does this describe a state of being, an attitude, or a mentality? Is it figurative or literal? Explain your answers.

4. Why can you "be in the Spirit" but not be in a trance, and yet if you are properly in a trance, you are "in the Spirit"? Explain the difference.

5. What is the purpose of trances and visions? Why does God use these things in our lives? Have you been in a trance or vision? Do you know someone who has? What have been the results of such experiences?

"We should not desire or seek visionary experiences
for their own sake, but for how they can help us draw
closer in deeper intimacy with our Lord. Lest we think
that supernatural trances were limited to biblical days,
I want to share…that trances from the Holy Spirit can be,
and are being, experienced by 'ordinary' Christians today"

(*The Seer*, Page 135).

As an "ordinary" Christian, do you
crave deeper intimacy with the Lord?

Examples of Visionary Revelation

AND THE SPIRIT LIFTED ME UP AND BROUGHT ME IN A
VISION BY THE SPIRIT OF GOD TO THE EXILES IN
CHALDEA. SO THE VISION THAT I HAD SEEN LEFT ME.

(EZEKIEL 11:24)

Lest we think that supernatural trances were limited to biblical days, [there are] testimonies of such experiences that date from closer to our own day....

Dr. Mahesh Chavda...tells how he took the final step to receive Christ as his Savior and Lord, becoming the first in his family to embrace Christ....Mahesh's account is an incredibly beautiful and accurate description of how the Holy Spirit brings a person into contact with the love and grace of God. Through the years since that night, Mahesh has been used mightily by God in a worldwide ministry of evangelism and healing and other miracles....

The life and ministry of Kenneth E. Hagin were profoundly influenced by his visions of Jesus....Dr. Hagin...describes how the gifts of the Spirit and, particularly, the gift of discerning of spirits, were in operation in him *only* when he was in the realm of the Spirit. In other words, it was not at his choice or volition, but only when he was, in his words, "in the anointing." ...

Maria Woodworth-Etter was a powerful evangelist and revival leader of the late 19th and early 20th centuries. Wherever she went, the power of God fell: people were slain in the Spirit, saw visions, received revelation, and were converted by the thousands.

(Quote from *The Seer*, Pages 135, 139-140)

The three people who are cited here have had profound experiences in visionary revelation. Use the chart below to trace their experiences. (Use the text of *The Seer,* Pages 135-142 to give you more information on each person.)

Person	Condition Prior to the Trance	Character of God Revealed Through the Trance	Results in the Person's Life and in the World They Touched
Dr. Mahesh Chavda			
Kenneth E. Hagin			
Maria Woodworth-Etter			

Studying your chart, can you see why God used trances to speak to each person and change their life? Do you think He desires to do the same for you?

MEDITATION

"Biblically and historically, the trance has been a legitimate method God sometimes uses to impart visionary revelation, and it continues to be so today.... Ultimately, God's desire is to bring us close to Himself and impart His will and His ways to us so that we can minister to others in wisdom because we have spent time standing in the council of God" (*The Seer*, Page 143).

God can impart His will and His ways to us in many different ways. Why, then do you think He uses trances to communicate to us?

Standing in the Council of God

BUT WHO HAS STOOD IN THE COUNCIL OF THE LORD, THAT HE SHOULD SEE AND HEAR HIS WORD? WHO HAS GIVEN HEED TO HIS WORD AND LISTENED?

(JEREMIAH 23:18)

The Lord gives vision to those who, in the words of Jeremiah, have "stood in the council of the Lord": …

But if they had stood in My council, then they would have announced My words to My people, and would have turned them back from their evil way and from the evil of their deeds (Jer. 23:22).

What does it mean to "stand in the council of the Lord"? …

Jeremiah speaks of seeing, hearing, giving heed to, and listening to the Word of God. Habakkuk refers to seeing an oracle and describes himself as a guard on the rampart keeping watch to see what the Lord will speak to him.…

In the prophetic realm, to stand in the council of God means both to see and to hear the Word of God. But for what purpose? Jeremiah 23:22 gives the answer: to announce God's Word to God's people in order to "[turn] them back from their evil way and from the evil of their deeds." In other words, the purpose of standing in the council of God is to produce fruit in the lives of God's people: the fruit of holiness, repentance, the fear of the Lord, and a godly lifestyle.

(Quote From *The Seer*, Pages 147-148)

QUESTIONS

1. What does the "council of the Lord" mean to you? Have you ever stood there?

2. Take the four components of the Jeremiah passage and explain how these work in your life. Do they all need to be present each time? Explain.

   Seeing—

   Hearing—

   Giving heed to—

   Listening to the Word—

3. How do seeing and hearing combine to bring obedience to the Word of God? Have they done so in your experience?

4. Do you think that every time someone stands in the council of God, fruit automatically appears in the lives of God's people? Why or why not? What principle do you see here?

5. Look at the four fruits mentioned above. Think about your experience in seeing and hearing the Word of God. Do these fruits easily come forth from your life? Do you share these with others?

   Holiness—

   Repentance—

   The fear of the Lord—

   Godly lifestyle—

"How can anyone 'see' what the Lord 'speaks'?
The simplest answer is that God has more than
one way of 'speaking.' His speech is not limited
to audible words or, indeed, to words of any kind"
(*The Seer*, Page 148).

Think about your answers to these questions.
What has your experience been…is it easier to hear or see?
Do you understand more clearly by sight or sound?

In Close Deliberation

ALSO WE HAVE OBTAINED AN INHERITANCE, HAVING BEEN
PREDESTINED ACCORDING TO HIS PURPOSE WHO WORKS
ALL THINGS AFTER THE COUNSEL OF HIS WILL.

(EPHESIANS 1:11).

The Hebrew word for "council" in Jeremiah 23:18 is *cowd*, which means "a session," or "a company of persons in close deliberation." It implies intimacy, as in secret consultation. By comparison, our English word "council" refers to a group of people called together for discussion or advice....

Just as there are earthly councils of men and women that come together to discuss and advise, there is also a council that takes place in Heaven, presided over by Almighty God, where we can hear and receive the *counsel* of the Lord—the wisdom and vision and direction that derive from the council of God. By His sovereign and personal invitation, we can enter God's "hearing room" to listen to the deliberation of His council so as to be able to announce His Word on an issue....

The Lord has revelation—secrets, if you will—that He wants to open up to us....One of the highest characteristics of a prophetic person is that he or she is supposed to be a trusted friend of God. God has secrets and He is looking for some friends to share His counsel with. It is an open invitation; we *all* can be friends of God.

(Quote From *The Seer*, Pages 148-149)

QUESTIONS

1. Compare the Hebrew meaning with our English word "council." How does it differ or become more distinct?

2. The "intimacy, as in a secret consultation" aspect of the Hebrew word infers what about the council of God? What would be the purpose of these being in secret?

3. What does Ephesians 1:11 mean by the "counsel of His will"? Who is at the council? Who gives the wisdom and direction from this council? How does the process of listening into the deliberation of His council help us?

4. What is the purpose of the council of God? What are we supposed to do after we have heard the counsel of His will?

5. Have you ever thought of God telling you His secrets? Have you ever felt you have heard something that was not to be revealed until a later time, or perhaps, not at all? To receive a "secret" from God, what disciplines do you need to exercise regularly?

"God's prophetic people are to be His friends.
They are to be the ones in whom He can entrust
His word, His message, and His revelation, often speaking
to them beforehand about what He is going to do"
(*The Seer*, Page 149).

*Why do you need to know what God says
ahead of the rest of the world? What purpose
would this serve? Ask the Lord to share more
with you so you can know what is and what will be.*

God Speaks Before He Acts

SURELY THE LORD GOD DOES NOTHING UNLESS HE REVEALS HIS SECRET COUNSEL TO HIS SERVANTS THE PROPHETS. (AMOS 3:7).

Why does God speak to His servants the prophets before He acts? Is God not sovereign? Can He not do whatever He wants to do without informing any of us? Absolutely, but God has chosen to work this way because at creation He gave the stewardship of this earth to the sons of men. He established a chain of command, so to speak. God has never rescinded His original decree giving mankind dominion over the earth. That is why He says, in effect, "Before I do anything, I will let someone—My friends—know what I am about to do."

God always acts with purpose. He reveals His secret counsel to us because we are His friends, but He also reveals it in order to get a job done—to accomplish His will....

As believers, we *are* God's friends—just as we are co-heirs with Christ—but our friendship with God is characterized by love as well as by faithful obedience and service. We find our identity not in who we are or what our title is, but in Christ and in servanthood. Who we are is not determined by what we do but in who we belong to. If we are "in Christ," our life is in Him. He *is* our life.

(Quote From *The Seer*, Page 150)

QUESTIONS

1. How does our job description as steward of the earth tie into the way in which God speaks to us before He acts? How are we capable of making changes, setting course corrections, and adjusting the way we operate due to pre-knowledge?

2. Have you ever heard God speak something to you before it happened, or do you know of someone who has experienced this? When God speaks this way, how are we to act upon what is spoken? Are we to alert people? Are we to do something different than we have been doing?

3. Because God always acts with purpose, why do we disavow His sovereignty when we credit circumstances to "coincidence" and "luck"? Why do we blame circumstances for so much of our misfortune? Why don't we readily ask God for understanding how He is using the circumstances to accomplish His will?

4. Looking at your answers to #3, how would you tell an unbeliever these things? How would you need to address the sovereignty of God that it might gain a hearing and not close the person off?

5. How is your friendship with God characterized—by love, faithful obedience, and service? If we are receiving the counsel of God, do we need to remain humble and ready to do what it takes to serve as needed? How do you intend to do this?

*"There are two sides to the coin of standing
in the council of God. On one side is the sovereignty
of God and on the other, the initiative of man.
One of the amazing truths of the Bible is
that the announced intention and counsel
of God can be altered by our intercession!"*
(*The Seer*, Page 150).

*Where are you in terms of the two sides
of the council of God? Are you able to merge the
sovereignty of God and the initiative you have
in your mind? In your heart? In your daily walk?*

Being There

Thus says the Lord of hosts, "If you will walk in My ways and if you will perform My service, then you will also govern My house and also have charge of My courts, and I will grant you free access among these who are standing here."

(Zechariah 3:7)

An experience of "being there" in the council of God is significant for several reasons. First of all, it is an honor when God grants this kind of audience. Second, the more subjective the experience, the greater the possibility of pure revelation. Finally, our own thoughts are out of the process, and reception in the spirit realm is in clearer focus.

These are important factors to consider because they help us establish the proper mind-set for walking in that realm. After all, if God grants us the privilege of such a supernatural encounter as standing in His council, we had better know how to act when we are there. God gives us instruction for this in His Word....

[Zechariah 3:7 has] God's conditions for standing in His council: "walk in My ways and...perform My service." This involves progressive steps of faithfulness. If we do those things, God promises that we will govern His house, have charge of His courts, and have free access to those who are standing there....

[There are] three important guidelines to help protect us from error during supernatural encounters...:

1. Avoid unhealthy familiarity and fascination with their personage....

2. Watch out for the issue of "commanding angels" in spiritual warfare encounters....

3. Be careful to use proper discernment in the distinction between the true angelic and the demonic counterfeit.

(Quote From *The Seer*, Pages 152-154)

✝

1. The significance of being in the council of God is threefold. Look at these and give input on each using the following chart:

Significance	The Mind-set This Helps Me Establish
The honor to be granted an audience.	
The more subjective the experience, the greater the possibility of pure revelation.	
The reception in the spirit realm is in clearer focus.	

2. How would you act if God granted you to stand before His throne at this very moment? Would you know what to say? What to do? How to follow heavenly protocol?

3. Look at the promises we can look forward to if we perform His service in progressive steps of faithfulness. Of these—governing His house, having charge of His courts, and having free access to those who are standing there—which is most exciting and why? Which are you most unsure of? Why?

4. The three guidelines to help protect us from error during supernatural encounters show what traps we need to avoid. Of these three, which would be the trap that might ensnare you the easiest? Why?

5. How do you intend to seek the counsel of God? What will put you in a position to be in the council of God and receive its benefits or promises?

"How then should we walk among those who are standing by in the council of the Lord? What should be our demeanor in His presence? The key—the only acceptable posture—is a spirit of humility in the holy fear of the Lord"
(*The Seer*, Page 154).

How do you enter the presence of God?
Does humility accompany your communion?

Giving Ourselves to the Process

"For I know the plans that I have for you," declares the Lord, "plans for welfare and not for calamity to give you a future and a hope."

(Jeremiah 29:11).

God is looking for people to share His counsel with. He is looking for people who have a passionate desire for Him. If our passion is for the Lord Himself—not visions or prophecies or manifestations or anything else like that for their own sake—then He will reveal Himself to us in any number of ways....God rewards all who seek Him with their whole heart....

Along with our passionate seeking, we must learn how to balance between the *objective* and the *subjective* experience. An objective experience is not determined by impressions, feelings, inner vision or voices, but is based upon convictions concerning God's character—His faithfulness to keep His promises. A subjective experience, on the other hand, is the cry of the soul for a clearer awareness of God; the passionate desire for a distinct hearing of His voice.

Whatever else we do, we must maintain our balance between the subjective and the objective. We must not become so fixated on prophetic or visionary revelation that we throw away the Bible. Let us keep our objectivity. The revelatory word is not a competitor with the written Word, but a complement to it, and *always* subordinate to it. The written Word of God is the unwavering standard by which *all* revelatory word *must* be measured.

(Quote From *The Seer*, Pages 159-161)

QUESTIONS

1. Jeremiah 29:11 tells us that God has only good plans for us. Is this easy for you to believe when you look at challenges you face in your life? Read verses 12 and 13 of the same chapter and meditate on the conditions for this kind of blessing.

2. When we are passionate to be with God, "He will reveal Himself to us in any number of ways." What are ways that God reveals Himself? What ones have you experienced?

3. "God rewards all who seek Him with their whole heart." What kind of rewards does God give us? What rewards have you received from the Lord?

4. Explain the balance between the objective and subjective experience. What are the limitations of each? What are the benefits?

5. How do the revelatory word and the written Word of God work together? Which is greater? Why?

MEDITATION

"Depending on their background and the teaching they have received in their churches, Christians respond to the phenomena of mystical experiences in different ways. Some are suspicious while others condemn and reject them outright. There are still others, however, who embrace these experiences, sometimes cautiously at first, then with increasing enthusiasm"
(*The Seer*, Page 161).

What has been your experience as to how Christians respond to mystical experiences? How have you embraced these experiences? Have you been cautious or enthusiastic? Think about how the Lord wants you to respond.

Hidden Streams
of the Prophetic

BUT WE ALL, **WITH UNVEILED FACE, BEHOLDING AS IN A MIRROR THE GLORY OF THE LORD**, ARE BEING TRANS-FORMED INTO THE SAME IMAGE FROM GLORY TO GLORY, JUST AS FROM THE LORD, THE SPIRIT.

(2 CORINTHIANS 3:18, EMPHASIS ADDED).

I have found that the most direct road to greater intimacy with God has come through the practice or discipline of an almost lost art...—something called contemplative prayer....

In contemplative prayer, we as Christians do not primarily relate to God as the one who sits upon His throne in Heaven but, through the reality of our new birth in Christ, connect with Him as the one who has taken up residence inside us. We each have a throne in our hearts where He dwells in a very personal way. In contrast, in intercessory prayer, we approach God who is seated on His throne in Heaven. We then, as priestly believers, make our appeal, stand in the gap, and remind God of His Word....

"Communion with God"...is commonly understood to mean coming into fellowship with God through the power of the Holy Spirit in Jesus Christ, who dwells in the born-again believer. Communion with God is a way of fellowshipping with the Holy Spirit by learning to quiet the distractions of our soul and of the world, calming the inner chaos and noise from outside that tends to vie so strongly for our attention....We come...into the heart or "center" of our being where God dwells through the Holy Spirit, who has taken up residence there.

(Quote from *The Seer*, Pages 163, 165)

1. Have you engaged in contemplative prayer? On a regular basis? What does the term "contemplative prayer" mean to you?

2. Think through the difference between intercessory prayer and contemplative prayer. How would you explain the difference to someone who is new in the prayer arena?

3. How does Second Corinthians 3:18 describe our journey of maturity? How does contemplative prayer help make the transformation?

4. Evaluate your "communion with God." Do you fellowship regularly through the power of the Holy Spirit through Jesus Christ? What is your fellowship with the Holy Spirit like—intimate and full, or staid and shallow? What can you do to grow in this area?

5. Describe the "center" of your being. How does God dwell there? Why does God choose to take up residence within you?

*"Christians tend to be divided into two camps.... One camp is the 'going and doing' camp, always going, always busy at the work, doing missions, serving the poor, and preaching the gospel. The other camp is the 'contemplative' camp, the meditative, quiet, and reflective ones who so love the 'interior castle' that they just want to dwell there and stay there all the time.... The **inner** life prepares us for the **outer** life; both are necessary. One of the lessons we must learn is to build a bridge between the two"*

(*The Seer*, Page 166).

Think about where you are in terms of these two camps. How do you need to bridge between the two?

Listen, Watch, Wait

NOW THEREFORE, O SONS, LISTEN TO ME, FOR BLESSED ARE THEY WHO KEEP MY WAYS. HEED INSTRUCTION AND BE WISE, AND DO NOT NEGLECT IT. BLESSED IS THE MAN WHO LISTENS TO ME, WATCHING DAILY AT MY GATES, WAITING AT MY DOORPOSTS. FOR HE WHO FINDS ME FINDS LIFE AND OBTAINS FAVOR FROM THE LORD. BUT HE WHO SINS AGAINST ME INJURES HIMSELF; ALL THOSE WHO HATE ME LOVE DEATH. (PROVERBS 8:32-36)

Communal prayer is not as much *doing* something as much as it is *being with* Someone, continuing in prayer with this Someone until we become the *expression* of Him in the world around us....

The eighth chapter of Proverbs provides three important principles related to contemplative prayer....Verse 34 contains the three principles: "listens," "watching," and "waiting." All three of these verbs are in the continuous passive tense in the Hebrew, meaning they are ongoing, rather than momentary. Blessed are those who listen and keep on listening, who watch and keep on watching, and who wait and keep on waiting....

Contemplative prayer is an exercise in letting go of the control of our own lives and no longer leaning on the props of the false self. It is a kind of communion intended to increase our intimacy with God and our awareness of His presence. It is a step of submission, where we place our being at God's disposal, as we request His work of purification. In Christ Jesus, we open ourselves up to the Holy Spirit to get in touch with the new man, the true self, and to facilitate an abiding state of union with God.

(Quote From *The Seer*, Pages 166-167, 169)

1. Explain communal prayer as you would to a person new to prayer. How does it bring one closer to God? How does it help the person become more the expression of God to our world?

2. What is your experience in communal prayer? Have you found it to be something that you seek to do often? Are your experiences rewarding and full? Have you found that it has changed you more and more into the image of God?

3. Look at the three principles in Proverbs 8:32-36. Of listening, watching, and waiting, which is easiest for you to do and why? Which is most difficult and why? What might you do to increase your capacity to listen, watch, and wait?

4. How does someone "let go" of his or her own life? What is the process to quit leaning on the props of false self? Have you experienced these to some degree? Explain.

5. How does submission enter into our communion? What impact does it have? Why is it a prerequisite to purification? Do you find that you embrace or endure submission? Why?

MEDITATION

"To 'contemplate' means to gaze at intently,
to think about intently, to study, to expect or
*to intend, to meditate, to muse. The word **muse***
means to think about, or to consider deeply, to meditate.
*To **meditate** means to plan, intend, to think deeply, to*
*reflect upon. The word **reflect** means to throw back light,*
heat, or sound, to give back an image as in a mirror, to
bring back or come back as a consequence or as reflected glory"
(*The Seer*, Pages 167–168).

Take time to muse, meditate, and reflect.
Give yourself a spiritual retreat, if even for a
part of a day and bring yourself into balance.

The Goal of Our Journey

FIXING OUR EYES ON JESUS, THE AUTHOR AND PER-
FECTER OF FAITH, WHO FOR THE JOY SET BEFORE HIM
ENDURED THE CROSS, DESPISING THE SHAME, AND HAS
SAT DOWN AT THE RIGHT HAND OF THE THRONE OF GOD.

(HEBREWS 12:2, EMPHASIS ADDED)

As we grow accustomed to the unifying grace of recollection, we are ushered into the second phase of contemplative prayer...called "the center of quiet," or the prayer of quiet.

Through recollection we have put away all obstacles of the heart, all distractions of the mind, and all vacillations of the will. Divine graces of love and adoration wash over us like ocean waves, and at the center of our being we are hushed, and there is a stillness, to be sure, but it is a listening stillness. Something deep inside of us has been awakened, and brought to attention, and our spirit now is on tiptoe, alert, and listening. Then out comes an inward steady gaze of the heart, sometimes called "beholding the Lord."...

[Another] phase of contemplative prayer is spiritual ecstasy....In that place of quiet detachment from the reality around them, illumination—the spirit of revelation—is granted and their being becomes filled with God's pictures, God's thoughts, and God's heart....Spiritual ecstasy...is not an activity or undertaking that we do, but a work that God does in us. Ecstasy is contemplative prayer taken to the nth degree....

Once we get to know these ways of Christ in us—the glory of God Himself living and dwelling in our being—and coming into union and fellowship with Him who now has taken up residence upon the throne of our lives, we will realize suddenly that we were created for that very thing.

(Quote From *The Seer*, Pages 171-173)

QUESTIONS

1. What is a "prayer of quiet" in your experience? Do you use this type of prayer in your devotional disciplines? How does it strengthen the unifying grace of recollection?

2. What does recollection do for the heart? What does it remove? What does it leave room for?

3. What does it mean to "behold the Lord"? Have you beheld Him? Does it seem ironic to you that you gaze inward and not outward to behold God?

4. How are contemplative prayer and spiritual ecstasy linked? Do you see why the church fathers wanted to get away in order to use these in their relationship with God? How can you come into contemplative prayer and spiritual ecstasy in today's hustle-and-bustle world?

5. What is the goal of your journey? How do you know you are moving in the right direction? What signs are there in your life?

6. How does it feel to know you were created for God to reside within you? How can you be sure He has taken up residence on your throne?

"Isn't [God] the goal of our passionate pursuit?
He is the stream of living water that makes my
heart glad! Let us pursue the "hidden streams"
of the prophetic and grow in greater intimacy with
the lover of our soul. He is the goal of our journey"
(*The Seer*, Page 174).

Is your journey steadily pulling you to God?
What course corrections do you want
to make on your journey?

The Key of Intimacy to Open Heavens

AFTER BEING BAPTIZED, JESUS CAME UP IMMEDIATELY FROM THE WATER; AND BEHOLD, THE HEAVENS WERE OPENED, AND HE SAW THE SPIRIT OF GOD DESCENDING AS A DOVE AND LIGHTING ON HIM.   (MATTHEW 3:16)

The baptism of Jesus was the occasion of another "open heaven" event....[Matthew 3:13-17] indicates that John as well as Jesus saw the heavens open and the Spirit descend as a dove, and he heard the voice from Heaven. This "open heaven" experience imparted to John information he would not have known any other way....The Spirit descending and remaining was the prophetic sign that enabled John to recognize the Son of God and to know that this man was different from any other man who had ever been born of woman....

How we need for "Jacob's ladder" to descend again, not just for one night, but permanently! So many of us are famished for the bread of the Spirit; let us call out for Him to come down not just to alight, but to remain, a manifested habitation of the Lord in our midst!...

What kind of person might have Heaven open above them? It would have to be someone who became radically undone in the Lord, someone who was absolutely "wasted" on Jesus.... Whenever Heaven opens over an individual, they carry that open heaven with them wherever they go and become climate-changers. They become history-makers.

(Quote from *The Seer*, Pages 178-180)

QUESTIONS

1. Meditate on the baptism of Jesus. Read Matthew 3:13-17 and see how John's life was changed by the experience. What changed?

2. Read Genesis 28:11-19. Think about the dream Jacob had when he was in such desperate circumstances. How did this dream change Jacob's life? In what ways?

3. Have you had Heaven open before you? If not, do you know someone who has experienced this? Is there a certain qualification a person needs before experiencing such a vision? Why or why not?

4. What are the results of someone who has had Heaven open over them? Are there only good results? What kind of life change does God expect?

5. Why does God let us have these open Heaven experiences? Of what use are they? What power can they bring to your life?

MEDITATION

"God is looking for candidates in this generation who will be seated with Christ in the heavenly places and call forth God's destiny and design into the earth realm. It has happened before in all historic awakenings. I am talking about ordinary folks who surrendered to an extraordinary God. I am talking about people like Charles Finney and Evan Roberts"
(*The Seer*, Page 180).

*Are you one of these candidates? If not,
do you want to become one?
Surrender to your extraordinary God!*

A Door in Heaven

AFTER THESE THINGS I LOOKED, AND BEHOLD, A DOOR STANDING OPEN IN HEAVEN, AND THE FIRST VOICE WHICH I HAD HEARD, LIKE THE SOUND OF A TRUMPET SPEAKING WITH ME, SAID, "COME UP HERE, AND I WILL SHOW YOU WHAT MUST TAKE PLACE AFTER THESE THINGS."

(REVELATION 4:1)

John the Beloved received an open heaven through which he saw the Lord. His experience came near the end of a long life of faithful and obedient service to Christ and His Church....

Once we see Him—once He really reveals Himself to us—we will be completely undone. When we see the One who is standing at the top of the ladder, we will be radically, totally wasted for Him! That is my goal—to see Him, to know Him, to become like Him; to become a *gate* for the sake of others....

Jacob saw One standing at the top of the ladder; John saw One sitting on the throne. This John—John the Beloved—is the same John who laid his head upon the chest of Yeshua the Messiah at the Last Supper; who heard the very pounding of the heartbeat of God; who heard the very breath of the Master, both in the natural and in the spirit realm as the *pneuma* or wind of the Holy Spirit. This John is the one known as "the disciple whom Jesus loved." John the Beloved is the only disciple mentioned by name who stayed with Jesus even to the Cross, after all the others had fled.

(Quote From *The Seer*, Pages 182, 184)

QUESTIONS

1. What was John doing when he received the revelation we have as our last Book in the Bible? His revelation was very detailed and very long. What do you think sustained him to receive all of the vision?

2. Are you in a place of intimacy in your life that God could give you such an intense revelation as John? Why or why not? What is needed to become this open? What was John's history to become this available for God's ultimate revelation? What is your history?

3. How does one hear the "pounding of the heartbeat of God"? How is it possible to hear "the very breath of the Master"?

4. Of John the Baptist, Jacob, and John the Revelator, who do you most identify with and why? Whose experience of an open door to Heaven do you most relate to?

5. If you had been John, what would have been your reaction to seeing such an array of pictures, creatures, and experiences? How would they change your life?

MEDITATION

*"Many believers are just after intimacy, while
many others are after souls. It is not an either/or
proposition. There is a bridge between them both,
a "leakage" between open heavens. A powerful vision
of the Almighty produces a passion for reaching souls.
Intimacy eventually leads to evangelism"*
(The Seer, Page 185).

*What kind of "leakage" are you experiencing currently?
Do you have enough "water" to leak?
Do you affect those around you?*

Open the Door

BEHOLD, I STAND AT THE DOOR AND KNOCK; IF ANYONE HEARS MY VOICE AND OPENS THE DOOR, I WILL COME IN TO HIM AND WILL DINE WITH HIM, AND HE WITH ME.

(REVELATION 3:20)

In Revelation 4:1 John says, "After *these* things I looked, and behold, a door standing open in heaven." After *what* things? Since the division of the Bible into chapters and verses was made long after it was written, it is only logical to look in the previous chapter to see what John was referring to. [Read Revelation chapter 2 and 3 to understand the context.] ...

[In Revelation 3:20,] whose door is Jesus standing before? This is a prophetic apostolic message, a heavenly message sent to a church in a city. It is not a word written just to an individual. Certainly, the invitation Jesus gives here applies to individuals, so it is quite appropriate to use this verse in evangelism as is so often done. Contextually, however, the word is for a group, a corporate body. Revelation 3:20 is an apostolic word about the voice of the Holy Spirit standing in front of a city....

Intimacy is the key that unlocks open heavens over entire cities. It has happened before and it can happen again. I firmly believe that it *will* happen again. Jesus did not stop knocking after Revelation 3:20 was written. He has been knocking for two thousand-plus years. Today, He stands at the doors of 21st-century cities, asking, "Who will answer?"

(Quote From *The Seer*, Pages 185-186)

1. How have you traditionally viewed Revelation 3:20's picture of Christ at the door? Does the context of this verse change the way you see it?

2. When Revelation 4:1 describes an open door...does it mean that He has opened the door or we have opened it? What does it take to open a door of Heaven?

3. Do you see yourself as a person who stands in the gate of a city to hear the invitation of Jesus? Why or why not? Do you think God wants you to become a door opener? In what ways?

4. How can your local church be a city-changer? How should you pray for the corporate Body of Christ for your city?

5. What will you do? Will you ignore the knock until He goes away? Or will you open the door and say, like Joshua, "As for me and my house, we will serve the Lord"?

*"So what is the purpose of **the seer**? Like all
true seers of old, we must reach high. We must look
heavenward. We must think otherly. We must
passionately pursue the God of visitation....May the
key of intimacy be put in the door of our hearts, families,
congregations, cities, and nations. May the prophetic
power of visions, dreams, and open heavens increase.
Because the seer's goal is to reveal the man Christ Jesus!"*
(*The Seer*, Pages 187-188).

*Are you a seer? If so, how will you increase
your availability to reach higher? If not, what will
you do to become available for this prophetic power?*

NOTES

NOTES

NOTES

NOTES

NOTES

NOTES

NOTES

NOTES

NOTES

Additional copies of this book and other
book titles from DESTINY IMAGE are
available at your local bookstore.

For a complete list of our titles,
visit us at www.destinyimage.com
Send a request for a catalog to:

Destiny Image® **Publishers, Inc.**
P.O. Box 310
Shippensburg, PA 17257-0310

"Speaking to the Purposes of God for This
Generation and for the Generations to Come"